261·1 BAR

Community va

Community value

Lynda Barley

CHURCH HOUSE
PUBLISHING

Church House Publishing
Church House
Great Smith Street
London SW1P 3NZ

Tel: 020 7898 1451
Fax: 020 7898 1449

ISBN-978-0-7151-4129-8

Published 2007 by Church House Publishing.

Cover design and typesetting by Fordesign, Surrey, CR0 3JR
Printed in England by Halstan & Co. Ltd, Amersham, Bucks

Contents

Foreword

Yesterday's orthodoxy was that as 'modernization' progressed, so the role of religion in society would diminish. Religion faced redundancy with the spread of greater prosperity and the most appropriate category for the churches where a handful gathered to worship was 'heritage'.

Yesterday's orthodoxy has disintegrated in the twenty-first century. The community value of places of worship is now better understood. Anecdote, however, carries the argument only so far.

It is very common to meet people, influenced by media coverage, who have a dismissive attitude to the work of the Church as national resource while being able to tell good stories about their local experiences. As this important book suggests, 'much of what the Church is doing in the community goes on below the radar'. The quality and the motivation for this work is only imperfectly captured in statistics, but our civilization is one in which numbers have a great authority and they are indispensable if government is to be enabled to appreciate and support the increasing contribution to social cohesion and regeneration being made by the churches.

Lynda Barley has assembled the facts in a very accessible way and in future there should be no excuse for missing the significant community value of churches – well beyond their primary purpose as places of worship. At the same time there is a challenge in these pages for church communities as we seek to make the best possible use of the opportunities that we have inherited.

There is a message of confidence and hope in this book as we recover our vision of a Church *for* England, whose DNA includes both a concern for the health of the whole community and a readiness to co-operate with others in addressing the complex reality of social fragmentation.

Richard Chartres
Bishop of London

Series introduction

A changing Church

> The Church of England is only beginning to grasp the scale
> of the social and cultural changes that have transformed
> its missionary context in recent years. British culture has
> changed and perceptions and expectations of Christianity
> and of the Church have changed with it.

These are the words of Bishop Graham Cray, introducing the recent
book, *Evangelism in a Spiritual Age.*[1] The Church's conversation with
our country must alter. For too long it has been one-sided, the Church
imagining people as it would like them to be, rather than listening to
where they are. Father Vincent Donovan, in his classic book, *Christianity
Rediscovered,*[2] described his attempts to introduce Christianity to the
Masai people in East Africa and spoke of the necessity of bringing the
gospel to where people are. He pictures a Church without uniformity,
specialization and centralization and asks how the Church should
respond to culture and so find new life in God. The consequences of
such a conversational approach for outreach and mission are highly
significant. Pope John Paul II suggested that relating Christ to culture
should be at the heart of evangelism. Yet, he observed that today
'countries with a Christian tradition are experiencing a serious rift
between the gospel message and large areas of their culture'.[3]

In this series of research-based booklets, we shall be listening and
seeking to discern the voices emanating from the shifting culture in
which the churches find themselves witnessing to Christ in the world
today. At the beginning of the twenty-first century in Britain, where
do churches alter their mission methods to the changing modern-day
culture and where do they stand apart? It was John Taylor, a former
Bishop of Winchester, who wrote that mission is about finding out

what God is doing and then joining in[4] and the present Archbishop of Canterbury has picked up this and made it a focus in our day. Sheffield diocesan missioner, Sue Hope (writing in The *Vicar's Guide*[5]) adds: 'learning how to interpret the Spirit, spotting the footprints of God in the earthiness of the ordinary life of a local community and following them into the unknown is at the heart of true mission'.

In various ways the religious tide in Europe has been changing radically since the Second World War. Successive Governments have, for years, been persuaded by religious sociologists that secularization was taking over. They are now recognizing the reality of a postmodern, religiously pluralist society where faith groups play an important role in community life. Christian churches remain a major feature in national life but the culture around them is fast-moving and diverse. 'A plural, post-modern, fragmented world – a sackful of conflicting world views – presents a huge challenge.'[6] If Christian mission is to mean anything in modern Britain, churches must learn from the example of the apostle Paul, who listened to the cosmopolitan society in the Athens of his day and responded to its challenge.

In western society, people have been said to 'listen with their eyes and think with their feelings' and much professional advice towards improving modern-day relationships is given on this premise. Listening skills have never been more vital to church life but we must listen not just to what people say, but to what they feel, what they show and what they do. Listening with discernment to people today, to their lives and their stories is the purpose of these research booklets. It is not too late for our churches to take time to listen, to be prepared to learn and to adapt to the messages they hear.

The recent report, *Mission-shaped Church*,[7] has struck a chord with many who feel the Church should be more responsive to the spiritual needs of those with no experience of church and those who have drifted away. Fresh expressions of church are being planted successfully across our land for young and old alike – some in unusual places.

At the beginning of the twenty-first century, the *missio dei*, the mission of God is guiding and leading us into particular new things while reminding us of the reassurance in the best of the traditional.

Opportunities in recent years to share some modern social and religious research findings have often been greeted with the encouraging response, 'so we need to reshape and revisit the basics'. The basics of our faith remain as relevant for our modern-day society as they ever were but the presentation and practice must change as society has changed. We need to regain our confidence in the spiritual and pastoral basics we offer a country that, in its turn, has lost its way.

WE NEED TO REGAIN OUR CONFIDENCE IN THE SPIRITUAL AND PASTORAL BASICS WE OFFER A COUNTRY THAT, IN ITS TURN, HAS LOST ITS WAY.

The road map for local churches today is fast-changing, diverse and rather bumpy. The Revd Andrew Cunnington recently wrote in his local parish magazine:

> Our church is changing and I feel as if we have the opportunity to be more like the church God intended – certainly more biblical in our character. We also have the opportunity to get weighed down and sunk without trace if we choose . . . Preoccupied by not enough money in the bank and not enough people in the pews and not enough people to get all the jobs done properly – that will sink us.

Many are beginning to feel that this is the modern-day challenge of God's Spirit to the churches in Britain.

Whether your church is a Rolls Royce model, a nippy Aston Martin, a family Ford saloon or a trusty transit van, my prayer is that the modern-day research messages brought together in this series will encourage you to take time to listen as God seeks to guide his Church along new paths. In recent years the importance of listening has come to the fore. Research is simply a systematic exercise in listening. When we listen and reflect on what we hear, we discover surprises that both encourage and challenge. This helps us to listen to what the Spirit is saying to the churches (Revelation 2 and 3), to look up to where God is evident in the world and behold his glory.

Lynda Barley

Church House, Westminster

Introduction

There is considerable searching in British society today. Many feel that the country has lost its way, lost its identity, lost its common life and that its people are seeking community, seeking somewhere to belong. Community life is not what it was. This booklet explores the fragmentation of community life in Britain today and finds people searching for community links that churches can provide. By 'Listening to the nation' and 'Listening to the local' we will hear the voices of those searching for the heart of community living and we will uncover the often hidden contribution local churches make to their neighbourhoods. We will discover that churches, far from being forgotten, are valued for the key role they play in community life.

'Listening to the past' will remind us of recent social changes that have brought relations between church and local society to where they are now. We see the relevance of sacred places in modern Britain and how churches frequently bridge social gaps in our neighbourhoods.

Finally, all this comes together to encourage churches to be relevant to the changing times. 'Surprising signs of the times' shares real stories of churches that have grappled with the changes in their neighbourhood. It will point churches not to withdrawal from modern-day pluralistic Britain but to greater participation, not to closed churches but to open ones, not to churches on the edge of community life but churches at the heart of their communities, to being church in the alternative communities of our times and bringing value to emerging community life again.

1

Listening to the nation

Prosperity at a cost

As a nation Britain has led the way in the world with social reforms and economic stability that have led to improvements in the quality of life of its inhabitants. But how is Britain doing now in the fast-changing world at the beginning of the twenty-first century? It remains one of the most prosperous nations in the world, for in the last half of the twentieth century Britain's economic growth averaged 2.5% a year. Personal prosperity is growing and our standard of living continues to increase. We consume more and enjoy a greater personal disposable income. In fact, personal disposable income has increased fourfold since the 1950s. The average family income now stands at £422 a week and the number of holidays taken abroad now stands at over 41 million, a sixfold increase since 1971.[1] Three-quarters of Britons say they have no material comforts missing from their lives, while living standards are projected to increase still further by one-third over the first ten years of this century.

Not only are we materially better off but we are also healthier. We live longer and stay active until later in life. In the UK today we have the second highest life expectancy in Europe, beaten only by the Swedes. Men can expect to live to 76 years of age, with the first 67 years spent in good health. Women can expect to live to over 80 years of age, spending 70 years in good health. The 2001 government census revealed that almost a quarter of households in England and Wales consisted of pensioners only. An expert in population studies at Stanford University, Shripad Tuijapurkar, has predicted that new anti-ageing treatments will

THREE-QUARTERS OF BRITONS SAY THEY HAVE NO MATERIAL COMFORTS MISSING FROM THEIR LIVES, WHILE LIVING STANDARDS ARE PROJECTED TO INCREASE STILL FURTHER BY ONE-THIRD OVER THE FIRST TEN YEARS OF THIS CENTURY.

soon see the average age of death increase further by a year every year. Whereas anyone reaching the age of 60 was considered to be near death's door at the turn of the twentieth century, it is barely old enough for retirement at the turn of the twenty-first century.

Across Britain better standards of living affect communities in different ways. Britain's population has broken through the 60 million mark but our towns and cities are projected to grow still more in size, in fact by 5 million by 2021, almost as much through increased longevity as through immigration. Britain, along with the rest of Europe, is ageing as the proportion of people aged 65 years or over is projected to increase to 20% by 2021, while the proportion of under-16-year-olds will be under 18%. This is particularly affecting our countryside, where already in these areas 18% are 65 years or over.[2] These areas are also more likely to be primarily communities of retired people, for across the nation economic participation of men aged 60 to 64 years dropped dramatically from 84% in 1975 to 50% in 1995,[3] although it has begun to increase again with pension concerns.

Faithful Cities, the recent high-profile report from the Commission on Urban Life and Faith,[4] looked at levels of economic prosperity in Britain and found rising inequalities that are well above the average in Europe. After adjusting for taxes and benefits, the ratio of the top fifth of household income in the UK is four times that of the bottom fifth. Experts claim, for example, that recent increases in gas and electricity prices mean that the cost of living for pensioners is rising faster than the official overall inflation rate.

Despite government distribution measures, household inequality remains effectively unchanged. The people of Sunderland earn on average only 60% of the incomes of families in central London, and to the west, the people of Truro earn 64% of central London incomes. The north–south divide continues to thrive but within 59 local authority districts there are greater income disparities than across the north–south divide. Neighbouring communities in Southwark, Milton Keynes and Preston each have wider income variations than between

Modern-day gated housing

the north and south of the country.[5] The government census revealed how different local communities only a short journey apart can be in terms of lifestyles, identities and experiences. We prefer to live among people who are like ourselves. Buildings where our property can be safe and separate from our neighbours attract higher prices. Gated estates are growing in popularity. 'Listening to the nation' has shown us an island Britain that is embracing modern-day living with relish but with little regard for the consequent segregation of its inhabitants into growing numbers of neighbouring islands.

Going it alone

The rise in 'individualism' at the end of the twentieth century is well charted by the European Values Study. Personal autonomy and self-development is valued highly in Britain today, with over half of adults in Britain believing that 'individual wealth can grow enough for everyone'.[6] It seems that Britain is a nation living for the here and now, striving for individual satisfaction in the expectation that this will of itself improve the common good. But the gap between the haves and have-nots is widening, and although most families are better off than ever, we still want more. The Future Foundation remarks:

> Our affluent society prioritises personal fulfilment and this culture fuels increasing and more diverse leisure participation . . . higher expectations of life are also adding to the sense of time-pressure . . . [and] the desire for self-development is increasingly seen as something work should provide.[7]

EARNING POWER HAS BECOME THE DEFINING HALLMARK OF SOCIAL STATUS.

Over three-quarters (78%) of us would rather carry on working and have money than work fewer hours for less pay.[8] In 1999 an NOP poll discovered that families spend on average £5,000 a year on getting people to do things they hadn't time to do themselves – childcare, cleaning, gardening, dog walking, ironing.

Whereas, in the past, work situations and social class defined communities, work is often now based elsewhere and earning power has become the defining hallmark of social status. Unemployment in Britain is low and a third of us enjoy the world of work; 85% enjoy socializing with work colleagues. Naturally, this takes us increasingly out of our local communities. A record number of women, 7 in 10, now go out to work, a rise from 56% in 1971. Working hours remain long and the number of pension-aged workers grew to 1.1 million in 2005.[9] Nearly one in four workers now works more than 45 hours a week but, interestingly, the same proportion work occasionally from home and 9% work there one or two days a week.[10] Working from home is most prevalent among the self-employed, managers and senior officials and is by its nature often a working environment separate from the market place. The changing world of work has created long, frequently solitary, working hours and commuter towns and villages that empty during the day.

Even when we are not at work, more of us are alone at home. At the time of the last government census 3 in 10 of all households contained just one solitary person, but this is projected to rise to approaching 40% by 2026. The majority of these are in older age groups; only 1 in 5 consists of adults under 40.[11] The number of lone parent households is also set to rise but at a rate in line with the overall increase, so remaining at around 10% of the total. The continuing increase in the number of households is causing concerns about its impact on the environment, but the social impact is just as challenging. Not only are older people increasingly living alone but nearly a quarter of dependent children in Britain live in lone-parent families, almost twice the proportion in 1981.[12]

EVEN WHEN
WE ARE NOT
AT WORK,
MORE OF US
ARE ALONE
AT HOME.

It is just 25 years since the invention of the first personal computer or PC, and in that time information technology has revolutionized our lives. We are becoming a nation of solitary people dependent on multimedia communication. Surfing the net has overtaken television as the favourite activity of web users in the UK. The average Internet user now spends $2^3/_4$ hours a day online compared with $2^1/_2$ hours watching television.[13] Often these activities happen at the same time. Shopping has become one of the most popular activities on the Internet, while Friends Reunited has become a global phenomenon for people of all ages.

Men and young people aged 16 to 24 years are still the highest Internet users, although one of the major national Internet providers recently promoted Silver Surfers week. To communicate today young adults use the mobile phone (48%), email (28%), Internet instant messaging (28%) with only 5% using pen and paper. Electronic media are means of communication that are here to stay. Broadband users, for example, spend an average of one full day a week using the Internet for a range of activities including email, games and online television, shopping, banking and phone calls.[14]

Seven in ten households have a personal mobile phone

ACROSS
BRITAIN
99% OF
HOUSEHOLDS
HAVE A
TELEVISION
AND AROUND
HALF OF ALL
LEISURE TIME
IS SPENT
WATCHING IT.

Across Britain 99% of households have a television and around half of all leisure time is spent watching it. 95% of households have a home telephone, 55% a home computer and 70% a personal mobile phone.[15] At the end of 2004 52% of households in the UK were online and 59% of adults used the Internet in the following three months.[16] Among children, 90% of secondary school pupils and I in 4 7- to 10-year-olds have a mobile phone. Advanced technological communication challenges how we relate to each other in our households, in our communities and in the workplace. It makes personal communication more remote and creates alternative communities. At the beginning of the twenty-first century the people of Britain have become a nation of islands where individual aspirations may have 'gained us the world' but at the expense of our social cohesion – and the cracks are beginning to show.

Faithful capital

If our communities are fragmenting, what is it that holds them together? In recent years the term 'social capital' has increasingly come to be used to identify the 'social glue' that unites communities. Social capital is the object of considerable debate and research, but broadly it refers to the way in which relationships and social networks contribute to the health of a community.

> People are enriched not only by their ownership of physical and financial assets or by the 'human capital' of their skills and qualifications, but also by their social relationships and participation in social networks.[17]

Working together for the common good contributes to healthy communities. At their best, churches and Christians, alongside congregations of other faiths and their adherents, contribute to the social capital found in our communities. The Commission on Urban Life and Faith calls this gift to community life from people of faith, 'faithful capital'. Faithful capital concerns community involvement and hospitality, human dignity and social justice, worship and prayer, values and transferable skills, hope and the celebration of life.

The theologian Professor Keith Ward refers to the threat from individual choice that undermines all bonds of social unity.

> The Church has a social and political role, to seek justice, but by sacrifice and reconciliation, not by hatred and violence . . . to serve the world in love and to proclaim in word and deed union with God's love for all, not just its own members.[18]

He concludes that across the twentieth century there was the realization that Christians are co-workers 'not to provide a secure path to heaven for a few who will escape the general doom of the world', but with the responsibility of making God's kingdom visible to our neighbours.

The contribution made by faith communities to civil society was assessed in an enquiry by the Northwest Development Agency in 2003. This survey of more than 2,300 faith communities across eight different faith groups powerfully demonstrated the important contribution they make to the region's social and economic life. Its twelve key findings can be summarized:

Faith communities are keen to be listened to

Faith communities are strongest where social need is highest

Faith communities are important custodians of built heritage

Faith communities bring visitors and tourists to the region

Faith communities offer social support services

Faith communities are active delivery agents of care in local communities

Faith communities are significant patrons of arts and sports

Faith communities stimulate unprecedented levels of volunteering

Faith communities have an important role in regeneration programmes

More could be done to involve faith communities

Faith communities are largely self-financing

Faith communities reach parts of society others can't

At points the report was able to quantify the significant contribution faith communities make to their local communities. Almost all faith groups allow other local community groups to use their premises. 45% of rural Christian churches were involved in support initiatives during the Foot and Mouth crisis. One in ten faith groups organizes or manages projects addressing a wide range of social issues while 14% organize environment projects, 51% organize football training and 33% fitness training activities in the community. Faith groups in the north-west bring an estimated 46,700 volunteers to community activities other than worship and 73% do not receive any public funding. Such contributions to the social capital of the region are a vital resource for local communities. David Blunkett, when Home Secretary, referred to faith workers (for example, vicars, ministers, priests, pastors, the Imam or Rabbi) as 'development workers', whether full-time, part-time, paid or voluntary. This is a resource available to all areas of our country.

CHURCHES CAN CONTRIBUTE FOR BETTER OR WORSE TO THE SOCIAL CAPITAL OF THEIR LOCAL COMMUNITY.

Churches can contribute for better or worse to the social capital of their local community. Their commitment and long-term presence can contribute positively to community cohesion and regeneration but they can also challenge short-term, outcome-driven projects. The faithful or religious capital they bring is unique. *Faithful Cities* argues that:

> religious faith is still one of the richest, most enduring and most dynamic sources of energy and hope for cities. Faith is a vital – and often essential resource in the building of relationships, and communities.

A recent William Temple Foundation research report entitled *Faith in Action* found that:

> where communities are increasingly broken or fragmented, religious capital offers wholeness . . . religious communities are seen as being far more connected with their communities than the government could ever be.[19]

9

It found that Britain is increasingly interested in and shaped by the values of faith and spirituality. The religious capital this brings has a growing influence, in contrast to the way a declining confidence in all institutions in Britain has affected perceptions of institutional religion.[20]

The parish system across our land provides a model of the Church's life that is hospitable. Every resident has a local parish church with which he or she can build a personal relationship. Parish churches facilitate the relationship between local churches and their neighbourhoods. Ann Morisy, writing in *The Vicar's Guide*,[21] reminds us that social capital involves the trustworthiness of relationships within a neighbourhood that can vary between neighbourhoods and even between streets in a neighbourhood. When trust breaks down anxiety is heightened and people move away. The neighbourhood becomes less stable, and this fragility of community life also has a negative impact on our churches. She challenges local churches:

> The loss of positive social capital over the last thirty years has been a significant contributory factor in the loss of energy in church life . . . If we are to grow churches, we have to grow community, and in this way we also grow the kingdom of God.

THE HUMBLE PARISH CHURCH IS OFFICIALLY 'AN ICON OF ENGLAND'.

A national treasure

The humble parish church is officially 'an icon of England'.[22] The Department of Culture, Media and Sport now includes it among its list of fifty-three icons nominated and voted on by members of the public. Churches have key roles to play in the hearts and minds of modern Britain. Their place in public life is beginning to re-emerge on both the national and local stages. Churches are increasingly valued for what they uniquely bring to our everyday lives.

'Churches make neighbourhoods better places to live.' So ran the headlines following a national survey in November 2005 on church buildings.[23] The survey revealed that almost 6 in 10 adults (58%) in

Britain agreed with the statement: 'places of worship make our neighbourhood a better place to live.' Agreement was highest (64%) among people living in areas of suburban/ urban fringe and lowest (54%) in commuter rural/ village areas. Even among young adults 55% agreed with this statement, and among those with no religious allegiance, agreement stood at 38%.

Places of worship make our neighbourhood a better place to live

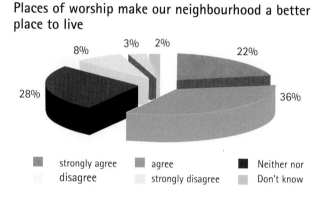

strongly agree   agree   Neither nor
disagree   strongly disagree   Don't know

How strongly do you agree or disagree with the following statement *(ORB 2005)*

6 IN 10 ADULTS (58%) IN BRITAIN AGREED WITH THE STATEMENT 'PLACES OF WORSHIP MAKE OUR NEIGHBOUR-HOOD A BETTER PLACE TO LIVE.'

So if our churches are valued across our towns, cities and villages by old and young alike, why are they so frequently underused? This national survey offered several other statements for participants to consider. Over 7 in 10 (72%) agreed with the statement 'a place of worship is an important part of the local community', and the same proportion agreed with the further statement 'places of worship provide valuable social and community facilities.' Not only did adults in Britain feel that churches make neighbourhoods better places to live but they were even more prepared to admit that churches were an important part of the local community and provide valuable social and community facilities.

Agreement for these statements was highest (74% and 76% respectively) among people living in either suburban/urban fringe areas or commuter rural/village areas. It was lowest (66% and 63%

respectively) among people living on council estates, but even here the result should encourage churches to contribute more in these areas. Among young adults 54% and 62% respectively agreed with these statements, while among those who had no religious allegiance agreement levels still remained at around half (56% and 46% respectively). The conclusion is clear. Where local churches make active contributions to their neighbourhoods the impact is valued.

This survey is the first to consider the role of our churches in modern neighbourhoods, and the results rebut the frequently heard assertion that the Christian churches in our communities are dead. Churches are alive and valued in local community life across our nation. Not only are they active and alive but local residents would like them to do more.

Over 6 in 10 adults in Britain (63%) think that 'places of worship should be more actively involved in our local community'. Even in our cities 60% agreed with this statement. Among young adults the level was similar (62%), while among those with no religious allegiance, agreement remained high at 41%. Not only should churches participate more in local communities but, it seems, they should be more accessible. Nearly 7 in 10 adults in Britain (69%) think that 'places of worship should be more accessible to our local community'. I am sure that this statement is not solely referring to government directives for disabled access, etc., though it no doubt includes these sentiments. What people are primarily asking for is open, welcoming and available churches in their midst. It seems that in all areas of the country, across all age groups and all faith groups, churches can play a more active role in community life. The survey revealed that 65% of adults living on council estates, 58% of young adults, 62% of people affiliated to non-Christian faiths and 48% of people with no religious allegiance want local churches to be more accessible to the local community. Listening to these findings the Bishop of London, Richard Chartres, commented:

NEARLY 7 IN 10 ADULTS IN BRITAIN (69%) THINK THAT 'PLACES OF WORSHIP SHOULD BE MORE ACCESSIBLE TO OUR LOCAL COMMUNITY'.

Churches are living, breathing communities reaching
out to churchgoers and non-churchgoers, central to
neighbourhoods and making possible much needed
and welcomed local facilities of all kinds.

These national survey results point our churches towards playing a
key part in local community life, but is this just limited to a social role?
For Christians their faith and social involvement goes hand in hand,
and churches would seek to maintain this dual role. Listening closer to
our nation reveals the perhaps surprising news that Britain today still
recognizes this connection and values its churches for it. A similar
national survey[24] run two years earlier discovered that by far the
majority of people, in fact over 8 in 10 adults (83%), saw their local
church first and foremost as a place of worship. Young people, city
dwellers and people with no religious allegiance all considered this
the most important role of their local church or chapel. Among young
adults 83% expressed this view, while among city dwellers the
percentage was 80% and among people with no religious allegiance
the percentage was 75%. Similar numbers saw it as a place for
baptisms, weddings and funerals (83%) and as a quiet space or
sanctuary (73%). Churches and chapels are primarily valued for
their religious or spiritual presence in our communities.

Over half of people in Britain also see their local churches as a local
landmark (59%), a historic place (53%) and a social/ community centre
(56%), but the chart below clearly shows that churches are primarily
thought of as religious or spiritual places in the community. Any social
involvement they have in community life is viewed in this context.

The relationship between the British and their churches was pursued
further in the same national survey. How concerned would people be
if churches were no longer present and what support did they feel
churches should have? The survey found that over 6 in 10 adults (63%)
agreed that they would be concerned if their local church or chapel
was no longer there, and this concern remained significant among
people with no religious allegiance (38%) and among people of

Churches seen as . . .

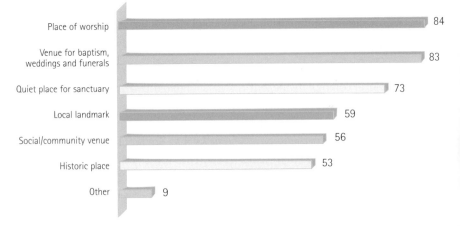

Place of worship	84
Venue for baptism, weddings and funerals	83
Quiet place for sanctuary	73
Local landmark	59
Social/community venue	56
Historic place	53
Other	9

How do you think of your local church/chapel? *(ORB 2003)*

non-Christian faiths (also 38%). One in ten did not know how the maintenance of their local church or chapel was funded, but 4 in 10 (42%) thought central taxation should contribute and 16% thought local taxation should contribute.

Concern for local churches and chapels is not hollow, for when this particular question was further refined in 2005 it was discovered that nearly 1 in 5 (18%) thought central taxation should be the primary funder, while another 8% thought that local taxation should be the primary funder. The National Lottery and English Heritage were also suggested as key funders alongside other voluntary support and regular worshippers. Over 1 in 3 (35%) felt that regular worshippers should have the primary responsibility of maintaining churches and chapels while 44% felt that regular worshippers should contribute to some extent. The Bishop of London listened again:

> The research clearly supports the Church's call for more
> state funding for the maintenance of not merely the
> country's architectural heritage but a central plank of
> its social cohesion.

Listening to the local

'Listening to the nation' has alerted us to the growing fragmentation within modern society and the unique 'social glue' that churches can provide. As we now turn to 'Listening to the local' we shall find more that contributes to community divisions. But we shall also see more of how churches contribute to community life for the good, the positive contribution that faithful capital engenders.

Happiness and Health 1950–2000

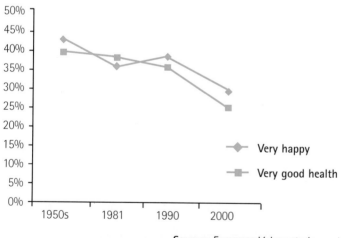

Source: *European Values study*

RESEARCH SHOWS THAT WHILE ECONOMIC PROSPERITY HAS INCREASED, HAPPINESS HAS NOT.

Striving for happiness

'Listening to the nation' has shown that we in Britain have never been better off or healthier, but the question is frequently asked, 'Are we happier?' For years politicians tried to persuade us that with a stronger national economy we would be happier, but research shows that while economic prosperity has increased, happiness has not. The European Values Study has tracked levels of personal happiness over the last half of the twentieth century and discovered that we actually feel less healthy and less happy than we did fifty years ago.

People in Britain are also generally less satisfied with life. The government Department for Environment, Food and Rural Affairs recently published quality of life indicators showing that two out of three households are unhappy with the levels of traffic, litter and vandalism in their neighbourhood. Crime levels have, in fact, gone down in recent years so there is considerable public debate about whether these anxieties are more imagined than real. What matters is people's perceptions, as researchers at Cardiff University found when they carried out a more thorough analysis of surveys going back 70 years.

'The good old 30s

It was the era of Depression, unemployment and poverty.

But we were happier then,' say researchers

The research found that people living in the 1930s were around 10% happier than those living in 2005. The surveys studied included how happy people were in relationships, how often they saw their family, how they fitted into the community and how they valued their leisure time. Professor Mansel Aylward, who led the research, remarked:

> We are more unhappy now than we were then . . . our
> expectations are greater. The most important ingredients
> for happiness are family relationships, family networks
> and a camaraderie which bring a sense of community
> and belonging. Also very important is belief in God . . .
> People who believe are happier than people who don't.

CommunicateResearch investigated this statement further and discovered that churchgoers are happier than those who do not attend church. In an online poll they conducted across Britain in January 2006, over half of the general public and those aligning themselves to the Christian faith felt they were happy in their life as a whole, whereas 7 in 10 of those who attended church at least once a month considered themselves happy.[1]

The New Economics Foundation has been at the forefront of recognizing that despite our economic prosperity, we do not necessarily feel happier with our lives. It is currently developing a well-being programme. The Foundation surveyed young people in Nottingham and found that a third were 'at the very least unhappy in life and may be at risk of mental health problems'.[2] A subsequent project among young people in urban Britain by the University of Bangor and the Children's Society reported that 52% often felt depressed and 27% said they had sometimes considered suicide.[3] Almost three-quarters liked living in their local area but only 20% felt that their area cared about young people. Substantial proportions of young people were concerned with growing vandalism, crime, violence, drug-taking and drinking in their area, but the research found that young people who had a religious affiliation, who prayed regularly and who had a sense of purpose, had more positive attitudes.

CHURCHGOERS ARE HAPPIER THAN THOSE WHO DO NOT ATTEND CHURCH.

Young people in Britain are under pressure. A quarter are living in lone-parent households and 21% are living in poverty. Britain has the highest rate of teenage pregnancy in Europe and, among adults, one of the highest suicide rates. The number of young males committing suicide has doubled over the last ten years and taken over from road accidents as the number one cause of death among 18- to 24-year-old men.[4] Young people are particularly vulnerable, and in a survey by the UK Medical Health Foundation in 2001 half of university students were found to show signs of clinical anxiety while more than 10% suffered from clinical depression. But depression is not just high among the young; business stress

levels around the world doubled over 2005 according to one business survey. This is partly due to the long working hours culture there is in many countries. Britain has longer working hours and shorter holidays than any other country in Western Europe. 40% of UK residents work more than 40 hours each week on average, with top managers being the biggest victims.[5]

BRITAIN HAS THE HIGHEST RATE OF TEENAGE PREGNANCY IN EUROPE AND, AMONG ADULTS, ONE OF THE HIGHEST SUICIDE RATES.

Modern-day living affects our home life, and that in turn also appears to be getting more stressful. Nearly 1 in 4 grandparents have experienced family breakdown in at least one set of grandchildren.[6] Family life is increasingly under the watchful eye of psychologists, who are now warning that it makes a difference to our well-being and our health. They report, for example, higher happiness levels among married couples than single people. It has even been suggested that a married woman looks two years younger and a married man one year younger than those who have not 'walked down the aisle'. Marital bliss has also been said to stave off influenza and be as good as a £72,000-a-year pay rise. Whatever the truth of the situation, the number of marriages is now beginning to rise again and the number of divorces has begun to decline[7] as we begin to see a higher value placed on marriage. 76% of adults in Britain today expect their marriage to last a lifetime,[8] although divorce is most common within the first five years of marriage and among couples in their thirties.

The reality of family life in modern Britain includes absent fathers, single parents, distant grandparents, increasing numbers of singles and childless couples. Many feel very alone, and the decline in neighbourliness we discovered in 'Listening to the nation' adds to their individual isolation. Up to half a million older people spend Christmas alone and more than a third of Britons suffer from loneliness, with women feeling more isolated than men.[9] For many of these loners there comes the additional problem of residential mobility. Around 10% of the population move home every year, 3 in 5 under 10 km and 1 in 8 over 200 km, mostly either for housing-related or job-related reasons. Professor Tony Champion researched trends in population mobility in Britain to find that rates are highest among young adults, lone parents, non-elderly loners, private renters and professionals.[10] Loneliness has been said to be the voice of the age.

Where you live in Britain apparently can make you more likely to be stressed and unhappy. YouGov conducted a survey in the summer of 2006 asking people how they felt about their jobs, home life and work-life balance. The survey discovered that living in the south-east was more stressful than any other part of Britain. People living here felt unhappy in their jobs and family lives and said they felt stressed, whereas people living in Devon and Cornwall might not be well off financially but they were more relaxed and content. Living in the Midlands produced low levels of stress, happiness at work but poor balance between work and home lives.

It was certainly not a normal week for the small Nottingham village, Harby, when it participated in a television reality show *The Week the Women Went*. All the women spent seven relaxing nights at Center Parcs while their husbands and boyfriends coped with domestic life without them. Afterwards when they reflected on the experience, the majority of the men felt it had brought them together as a community. Their testimony is a challenge to modern-day Britain, where so many live fragile, separate lives in separate communities. They appreciated the opportunity to get to know each other and now they feel

> the spirit in the pub is amazing, it's like going back to what the village used to be like 30 years ago.[11]

The way we live today makes it harder to put time and effort into knowing people, but in Harby the men had to cope together, their friendships grew and community life grew.

Happy to belong

Modern-day living is often transient, but within most of us is the need to belong in some way. The British Social Attitudes Survey found that in 2001 nearly two-thirds of people belonged to at least one social network.[12] The most popular are a sports group, hobby or leisure club (40%) and churches or religious groups (25%). Interestingly, these membership figures are split into those who have taken part (38% of sports groups etc. members and 19% of church members) and those who are members but have not taken part (2% among sports groups and 6% among churches). Across all the social networks considered (sports, religious, charitable, neighbourhood, unions, political and other social) women were more likely to participate than men and, although sports groups are included, older age groups were more likely to participate than younger age groups.

Organizational membership and participation *in previous 12 months*

	Member, has taken part	Member, has not taken part	Not member
Sports, hobby, leisure club	38%	2%	51%
Church or other religious organization	19%	6%	64%
Charitable group or organization	14%	3%	75%
Neighbourhood group or organization	8%	3%	75%
Trade union or professional association	6%	15%	67%
Political party, club or association	4%	1%	81%
Association or group not listed	14%	2%	71%

Source: British Social Attitudes 2002/3

In the same year, the Church Life Profile, a nationwide survey of regular churchgoers was completed by Churches Information for Mission. Only 9% of regular churchgoers across all the Protestant denominations reported that they had no sense of belonging to their local church, and for nearly a half (49%) their sense of belonging was growing.[13] Among Anglican churchgoers, in particular, the figures were very similar. 10% felt no sense of belonging while 46% felt their sense of belonging was growing. One of the ways that many church members get involved in the life of a church-based community is through small groups and social activities. 57% of Anglican regular churchgoers and 69% of other Protestant regular churchgoers are involved in group activities of one sort or another in their local church. These are almost equally split between those that are purely social in nature and those that focus on faith development.

When Richter and Francis in 1996 explored the reasons given by church leavers in Greater London for leaving church, they discovered that half 'did not feel a part of the church'.[14] This proportion increased to nearly 6 in 10 (58%) among young people under 20 years of age. A quarter said, 'there were cliques or "in-groups" from which I felt excluded', although this view was less common among younger adults. Belonging is an important part of church life, and when this is absent this research showed that many drift away. This survey of church leavers concluded with the disconcerting finding that '92% of leavers reported that no one from the church had talked with them while they were attending less frequently, during the first six weeks after their churchgoing dropped off.' A critical period when re-engagement was possible had been lost in nearly all cases.[15]

These results are backed up by a further study, this time among regular churchgoers, which found most people who stop attending church do so because they have had a dispute with a fellow member of the congregation.[16] The study in 2005 discovered that people are more likely to leave church because of irritations with

PEOPLE ARE MORE LIKELY TO LEAVE CHURCH BECAUSE OF IRRITATIONS WITH OTHER CHURCHGOERS OR THE STYLE OF CHURCH MEETINGS THAN BECAUSE OF RELIGIOUS DOUBTS.

Community value

other churchgoers or the style of church meetings than because of religious doubts. In the companion booklet *Christian roots, contemporary spirituality* we examined the success of the Back to Church Sunday campaign initiated in the Diocese of Manchester. The campaign is aimed at those who have drifted away from church, and when the churches involved in the 2005 campaign were surveyed they reported that 1 in 5 of those who returned to church on this particular Sunday were invited by a friend. One of the most worthwhile things our churches can offer people in Britain today is the opportunity to belong to a local community, but the social glue in any community involves effective, durable relationships. Churches that give attention to the pivotal role of individual relationships will find they are building stronger communities.

CHURCHES THAT GIVE ATTENTION TO THE PIVOTAL ROLE OF INDIVIDUAL RELATIONSHIPS WILL FIND THEY ARE BUILDING STRONGER COMMUNITIES.

The Church Life Profile survey in 2001 investigated this in more detail. Again, 1 in 5 regular churchgoers admitted that the first prompt to join their local church was an invitation from a friend or family member.[17] People are instrumental to our sense of belonging and yet, in the same survey, 1 in 5 regular churchgoers admit they rarely, if ever, welcome new arrivals into their church. In addition, half said they were not likely to take time to talk with people drifting away from church. These results support the findings of the Richter and Francis study. Many people drift into and out of our churches with little personal contact being made. Maybe if we realized how welcome the community life offered by our churches can be to our neighbours we would be more confident in welcoming and caring for new church attenders. The Revd Alison Gilchrist, in a booklet on the church and hospitality,[18] encourages local churches to emulate the fast food chain McDonalds by offering a warmer and more professional welcome to strangers. Certainly, if we took more time to provide a welcoming open door and a less open back door, churches would be stronger community centres in our neighbourhoods.

Open churches

Local churches may or may not be physically at the centre of neighbourhoods across Britain, but 'Listening to the nation' has shown us that they are used by local residents for a variety of purposes and are valued for the key role(s) they play at the heart of communities. In fact, only 1 in 7 (14%) of adults in Britain have not been into a church or place of worship in the past year.[19] The figure rises among adults in their late twenties and early thirties but only to nearly 1 in 5 (19%). It rises to similar proportions (18% and 17% respectively) among people living on council estates and among people with no religious allegiance and, as may be expected, is at its highest (27%) among people of other (non-Christian) faiths. Churches are used on a regular basis by all ages, all faith groups and all types of neighbourhood. Not only was this the case in 2005 but previous research had revealed the same story in 2003 and 2001. At the beginning of the twenty-first century a staggering 86% of adults in Britain use local churches in some way as part of their everyday lives (at least once a year).

Our local churches are tremendous community resources to which people refer at key points of their lives. In the past year half of the adult population has attended a church or place of worship for a funeral, half on the occasion of a wedding and half for a memorial service for someone who has died. 4 in 10 attended at Christmas, 4 in 10 for a christening/ baptism and 4 in 10 for a social/community event. 3 in 10 attended at Easter, 3 in 10 for Remembrance Sunday, 3 in 10 for a concert or theatrical performance and 3 in 10 for a normal Sunday service. 2 in 10 attended for harvest celebrations and 2 in 10 through their children's school, but perhaps of most interest are the 2 in 10 who find in their local churches and places of worship a quiet space.

More than 2 in 10 people admit they were 'walking past and felt the need to go in', while almost the same proportion attended specifically 'to find a quiet space'. In our busy, noisy modern-day

AT THE BEGINNING OF THE TWENTY-FIRST CENTURY A STAGGERING 86% OF ADULTS IN BRITAIN USE LOCAL CHURCHES IN SOME WAY AS PART OF THEIR EVERYDAY LIVES (AT LEAST ONCE A YEAR).

Reasons for attending church in the year 2005

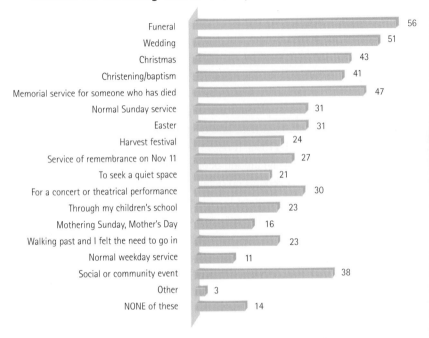

Funeral	56
Wedding	51
Christmas	43
Christening/baptism	41
Memorial service for someone who has died	47
Normal Sunday service	31
Easter	31
Harvest festival	24
Service of remembrance on Nov 11	27
To seek a quiet space	21
For a concert or theatrical performance	30
Through my children's school	23
Mothering Sunday, Mother's Day	16
Walking past and I felt the need to go in	23
Normal weekday service	11
Social or community event	38
Other	3
NONE of these	14

Thinking about the last year, have you attended a church/place of worship on any of these occasions? *(ORB 2005)*

world our churches provide welcome places of quiet refuge where people can be still and alone with their thoughts, concerns and personal prayers. In city areas the need is greatest, with 3 in 10 dropping in for a quiet space, and yet here it is often harder for churches to provide this opportunity. Open churches must be our aim but security implications need to be specifically managed. Even among young adults and people with no religious allegiance the use of churches as quiet spaces remains high. In the companion booklet *Churchgoing today* the pop singer Rod Stewart was quoted as using open churches in this way to 'go in and have a prayer', with the added challenge that in today's world this is seen by many to be 'churchgoing'.[20]

'Listening to the nation' and 'Listening to the local' have shown us that the pressurized demands of modern-day living affect us all, and the problems that affect individual lives are, if anything, increasing. When national opinion polls concerning church attendance were repeated in 2001, 2003 and 2005, regular attendance at ordinary church services remained static[21] but the range of occasions on which people attended churches or places of worship increased dramatically. In the past year 86% of adults in Britain have attended a church or place of worship on some occasion, and from the 18 different types of occasion described, these church attenders identify an average of $5^1/_2$ undertaken in the previous year.[22] In 2003 and 2001, 86% and 84% respectively attended a church or place of worship in the previous year and from 17 options provided, they identified on average $4^1/_4$ different occasions.

OPEN CHURCHES MUST BE OUR AIM BUT SECURITY IMPLICATIONS NEED TO BE SPECIFICALLY MANAGED.

Not only are our churches being used for an increasing range of community occasions but the proportion attending each of the different types of occasion is increasing. Funerals, weddings, baptisms, Christmas, Easter, Harvest, Remembrance services, memorial services, social and community events, concerts and theatrical performances etc. all attracted steadily increasing numbers of people over 2001, 2003 and 2005 when the national surveys were carried out.

The number of people using churches and places of worship as quiet spaces increased steadily from 1 in 8 (12%) in 2001 to 1 in 5 (19% and 21% respectively) in 2003 and 2005. More dramatically, the proportion who were 'walking past and felt the need to go in' increased from 1 in 11 (9%) in 2001 and 1 in 8 (13%) in 2003 to nearly a quarter (23%) in 2005. What opportunities open churches present! They are valued as points of connection with the everyday lives of our neighbours and are being used by communities on an increasing number of occasions.

Reasons for attendance

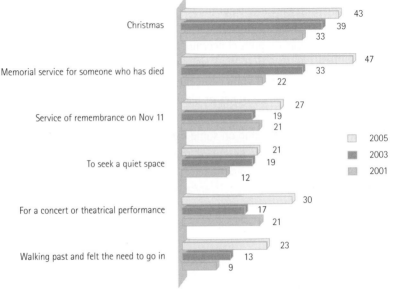

Thinking about the last year, have you attended a church/place of worship on any of these occasions? *(ORB 2001/2003/2005)*

Community life

The North Yorkshire Church Tourism Initiative is perhaps unique. It arose from research into the feasibility of developing a Christian heritage trail in North Yorkshire and attracted funding from the Heritage Lottery Fund, Yorkshire Forward, the Countryside Agency, the Open Churches Trust, local authorities and the National Park authorities. The research commissioned by the Churches Regional Commission for Yorkshire and Humber and the Yorkshire Tourist Board found that half of churches in the county were regularly open to visit, and many other churches had a notice displayed telling visitors where they could get a key. It suggested that a rural church typically attracts 1,000 to 4,000 visitors per year. The four-year tourism initiative that followed supported 117 church-based projects and over 30 workshops and information sessions. Visitor numbers at the 285 churches that participated across a number of denominations (measured by the number of actual signatures in the visitors' books) rose by 120% between 2000 and 2004/5, the greatest volume coming from within Yorkshire and the Humber.[23] Not only did the initiative succeed in increasing the contribution churches make to tourism but it built links between the churches and their wider community, encouraging churches to provide a more effective ministry of welcome to visitors. A Churches Heritage Officer has subsequently been appointed for East Yorkshire with the support of government funding from the Department for the Environment, Food and Rural affairs, and various partnership projects have begun, including the appointment of a culture officer by the Churches Regional Council. The survey revealed that visitors frequently visit more than one church, so challenging churches to work together.[24] When churches seriously engage with tourism this study shows that the relations with the surrounding communities are significantly enhanced.

In 2005 the Derby Diocesan Council for Social Responsibility set out to discover the nature and extent of faith group activity in Derbyshire communities. With the support of the government ChangeUp Framework, Churches Together in Derbyshire and the Derby Forum of Faiths a survey of all Christian denominations and other faith groups across the county was undertaken. Nearly half the questionnaires were returned completed and a number of representative case studies were examined. Their general findings[25] were that faith is a motivator to community action and that faith groups contribute to their community regardless of the number of weekly attenders. Activities covered a wide range, from individual visiting and support in the home, various arts and sports, children's and youth groups, parent support groups, credit unions, work on management committees, supporting marginalized people to running schools or shops. All age groups were covered by these activities, and often mixed age groups attend together. Beneficiaries of these services were not solely church or faith group members.

IN 2001, 2003 AND 2005, REGULAR ATTENDANCE AT ORDINARY CHURCH SERVICES REMAINED STATIC BUT THE RANGE OF OCCASIONS ON WHICH PEOPLE ATTENDED CHURCHES OR PLACES OF WORSHIP INCREASED DRAMATICALLY.

Contribution of the churches to community activity

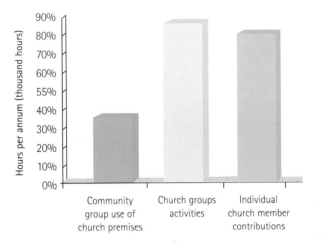

Source: *Faith in Derbyshire, Derby Diocesan Council for Social Responsibility (April 2006)*

When the Christian faith findings were examined separately it emerged from the Derbyshire study that a quarter of volunteers in church-run activities were not church members themselves. Churches significantly contributed to community life through their various buildings, with 45% of premises linked to the responding churches being used by other community groups for 35,000 hours per annum. Individual church members and church groups/activities each contributed more than double these hours. Assuming the average wage for Derbyshire in 2005, the responding churches contributed more than the equivalent of £1.4 million per year in church-run and individual community activities, which, when extrapolated across all the churches, was estimated to be worth over £5 million per annum.

The Derbyshire audit of community involvement also sought to assess the support needed by faith-based voluntary and community groups and to increase opportunities for partnership working. It found that 48% of churches would like to develop the community use of their premises and made a number of recommendations to assist the support of workers and access external funding. The exercise not only assessed the huge impact that faith groups were making in their communities but is being used to encourage further community partnerships across the county.

Various regionally based appraisals have been made in recent years by ecumenical church groups to measure the contribution of faith groups to social action and culture. The Brighton and Hove Churches Community Development Association, however, sought to effect a more localized study by mapping community involvement by Christian groups in its area. It discovered 120 Christian congregations or voluntary organizations running 301 community activities, groups or projects. Of the 55 community buildings identified as essential to the provision of services and facilities, 47 were church halls and worship spaces provided by the churches themselves.[26] The survey attempted to identify and interview every Christian congregation and voluntary organization in Brighton and Hove. It achieved interviews with 83% of these and concluded:

MUCH OF WHAT THE CHURCH IS DOING IN THE COMMUNITY GOES ON BELOW THE RADAR.

> Many groups and projects are not seen as part of the voluntary and community sector. Much of what the Church is doing in the community goes on below the radar. It is easy to underestimate the Church's contribution to the community in terms of supporting other voluntary and community groups, schools and other service providers, whether that be corporately or individually.

Local community audits can also be a useful means by which a neighbourhood mapping can be established. Dr Greg Smith of the Aston-Mansfield Communities Involvement Unit established a Newham directory of religious groups in 1999.[27] In the Newham area of London alone his fieldwork uncovered approaching 300 different religious groups. 225 groups (of a total of 294) were Christian, in turn dominated by Pentecostal congregations. Over 350 full-time staff were employed, although fewer than half were religious leaders, and at least 104 buildings were owned, while other groups rented the building in which they met. 620 activities and groups in addition to public worship were provided by the groups in Newham's religious sector, about a third of these open to the wider community. The most common types of 'secular' activity open to the wider community were social support of pensioners, parent/toddlers etc., uniformed organizations, community language classes, housing and child care.

Such neighbourhood mapping exercises can be utilized alongside a community survey to assess priorities of need in the local population and discover gaps in local service provision that local churches might engage with in local partnerships. Wakefield Cathedral did this as part of its Mission Audit in 2000.[28] Fresh Expressions commend this as an ingredient to their recommended local mission audit process.[29] The Barking Road Community Audit in Plaistow and Canning Town, London is one area where Greg Smith has successfully carried this out.[30] With funding from the Church Urban Fund and local charities, this community audit set out to discover the views of local residents. Existing population demographic statistics from the most recent government census and other sources were used alongside a survey of local residents and focus groups of key sectors of local young people and adults. Several key opportunities and unmet needs emerged, including those involving refugees and arts/culture.

Perhaps you are considering a community audit where you live. Recently the author worked with the Commission on Urban Life and Faith and the Church Urban Fund to establish a toolkit for local churches to assess the social capital they bring to their neighbour-hood.[31] The Churches Community Value Toolkit is ecumenical and is designed to highlight the ways in which churches contribute to their community. The hours of voluntary and paid work that spill over into the community are quantified so that churches and local decision makers are encouraged to value the role of local churches in community life and assess the financial value of their contribution to the wider community. The toolkit (and spreadsheet) also enables

churches to note some of the ways in which their contribution to
the local neighbourhood might be distinctive, for there are unique
contributions that faith can make to the well-being of a community.
It is a measure of its success that the toolkit is being enhanced to
consider more fully the often more informal involvement of the
church in the lifeblood of rural village life. Increasing numbers
of churches are finding such toolkits useful to establish a 'baseline'
and identify changes over time. Requests for funding and grant
applications frequently require such supporting evidence and
measurable outcomes. When churches pause to consider the faithful
capital they contribute to their local neighbourhoods, they usually
discover an encouraging surprise.

3

Listening to the past

A way of life

People in Britain today have lived through significant social changes in their own lifetimes. Many older people were brought up with church or Sunday school connections that are not commonplace today for themselves, their children or their grandchildren. We need to listen to the past experience of church within the lifetimes of many alive in Britain today so that we can more fully understand the inherited role of our churches in the heart and soul of the nation. One particular story serves to illustrate how church involvement in community life has evolved in recent years.

Local historians say that the Whit Walk in Kingswood, near Bristol, has been held every year since the end of the eighteenth century. The beginning of the procession has been linked to the founding of Sunday schools in East Bristol and Kingswood but, since 1945, the Walk has been organized by the Kingswood and District Christian Council Children's Committee, which is composed of representatives from each of the local churches and chapels and their Sunday schools.

Over 20 churches and chapels took part in 1988, seven bands played, there was a mounted police escort and about three thousand marched. Every year each church and chapel contributes between forty and three hundred people to the procession: children on floats, clergy, wardens and elders, mission bands, members carrying decorated banners representing the church, chapel or church organization.

The Whit Walk, though, is far more than a Sunday school parade, for the local newspaper estimated that ten thousand watched in the rain in 1985.

> All Kingswood is there . . . It is a family event, both in the
> sense that people meet up with relatives and in that it
> repeats a pattern [across generations] . . . It is also a local
> event, in that the participants are immersed in the crowd,
> and through this in the history of the area . . . [It is] a
> celebration of local identity.[1]

In more recent years, then, the Whit Walk has become a walk of
Christian witness demonstrating the unity of the local churches. It
has evolved into a popular festival or celebration ending in a fête at
the parish church which, for some years, has involved competitive
games. So why does this community event still attract such support
and local involvement on such a significant scale after all these years?
The Revd Dr Timothy Jenkins rigorously examines this question in his
appraisal of religious practices in English everyday life.

He concludes that two different worlds are celebrated and come
together in the Whit Walk. Alongside the churches and chapels of
Kingswood has evolved a parallel, separate sphere of community life.
Chapel activities, social functions etc. involve many on the edge of
chapel life, many friends and neighbours, and slowly these have
developed a life of their own. Jenkins found that this organizational
life 'never joins up with that of chapel life, not only because it has a
wider, more diffuse focus, but also because its leadership is recruited
from among its own members, who may never have had any other
contact with the chapel'. Even children in Sunday school often became
teachers, attended adult activities and finally became members of old
people's clubs while staying outside the chapel.

The Whit Walk, then, brings together the parallel local worlds of
chapel and church, their connected community and their friends and
neighbours. The Church in Kingswood has been and continues to be
instrumental in the celebration of local community life but its role has
changed markedly from the days when it founded the Sunday schools
and other chapel activities.

Jenkins moves on to examine further different roles of church in community life as he studies St Mary's, Comberton, a medieval country church near Cambridge. In the nineteenth century the church organized the schooling of the parish's children along with other provident societies that made it a part of a well-defined patronage system. However, as the role of the rural clergyman became more involved with landowner and magistrate duties, he became increasingly distant from his agricultural parishioners and lost any monopoly of interest in village welfare and education. This separation of church and civic life continued a trend established in the nineteenth century, when charitable and welfare provision began to be made by the government rather than the churches.[2] Churchgoing was becoming more and more separate from village life and faith was becoming increasingly the vicar's job, not that of local residents. Some saw it as 'involving as many as are willing in the life of the church', while others saw the church as 'having a role with respect to the village conceived as a community'. The former, more modern and urban focus invites the community to participate in local church life, while the other, more rural, perspective encourages the church to participate in local community life. Two different but complementary views have come to steer the involvement of local churches in their surrounding communities.

Various studies have charted the continuing differences in religious participation in rural and urban communities.[3] What is clear from these studies is that clergy have generally become less in touch with local congregations and communities, churches are used less and open less, in short the church has become less involved in community life. In both rural and urban situations, though held together by the parish system, what had been its strength is now increasingly stretched.

Sunday schools then and now

Sunday schools, in particular, have been a way of life for many who were brought up in Britain over the nineteenth and twentieth centuries, but their changing fortunes make for interesting reflection as we consider the changing role of churches in community life. At the beginning of the nineteenth century there was one Sunday school for every 2,130 people but by 1851 there was one for every 745 people.[4] In contrast and despite rapid building, there was approximately one church or chapel for every 770 at the beginning of the eighteenth century but only one for every 1,275 people in 1851. By this time almost two-thirds of Sunday school enrolments were non-Anglican, but as the twentieth century proceeded, the proportion of Anglican enrolments grew.

In examining this period, Professor Robin Gill shows that the number attending Sunday school continued to grow until the early twentieth century, when it reached a peak of more than half the eligible population. Whereas at the beginning of the nineteenth century 12% of those under 15 years of age were enrolled at Sunday school, a hundred years later the proportion was 52%. However, Gill goes on to show that although this pattern persisted between the two World Wars of the twentieth century, it changed very quickly afterwards. By the 1960s only 1 in 5 (20%) of children under 15 attended Sunday school.

> Between the wars . . . most children went to Sunday school, but most of their parents did not go to church. After the Second World War this pattern changed significantly: most children did not go to Sunday school, nor did their parents go to church.

A fundamental way of life involving churches in their local communities was changing and with it many community connections dwindled.

Bridging social capital

To understand further the evolving relationship between church and people, we must now look to America, where the churches' role in community life has for some time been a subject of much interest. Professor Robert Putnam, in his landmark volume *Bowling Alone*,[5] chronicled the decades of decline in sociability and civic participation since the 1960s across the United States. The decline in religious participation is well known, although church membership and attendance levels still exceed those in Europe. Putnam paints a broader canvas as he demonstrates how not only church membership but membership of team sports, social clubs and unions, involvement in civic associations, participation in public affairs, time spent with family, friends and neighbours, philanthropic giving, trust in others and even the widespread and intergenerational bowling leagues (from which the book takes its title) have all fallen by 25% to 50% over the previous three decades. Putnam goes on to show rigorously how a variety of technological, economic and social changes, for example, television, two-career families and the urban sprawl, has significantly reduced America's stock of social capital.

YOUNGER GENERATIONS STILL HAVE STRONG TIES TO FAMILY, FRIENDS AND CO-WORKERS BUT THEY FEEL 'LESS CONNECTION TO CIVIC COMMUNITIES – RESIDENTIAL, RELIGIOUS, ORGANISATIONAL . . . [THEY] ARE LESS EMBEDDED IN COMMUNITY LIFE'.

Putnam's investigation into different generations is particularly revealing. He refers to those born before 1946 as 'an unusually civic generation'. Younger generations still have strong ties to family, friends and co-workers but they feel 'less connection to civic communities – residential, religious, organisational . . . [they] are less embedded in community life'. Younger generations are less involved in both religious and secular social activities than were their predecessors at the same age. Religious involvement, Putnam demonstrates, is a crucial dimension in civic engagement and both are closely tied together. But as church attendance has lessened, so has the engagement of churches with their communities. One of Putnam's conclusions makes stark reading:

Trends in religious life reinforce rather than counter-balance the ominous plunge in social connectedness in the secular community.

Research in this area in Britain has been slow to develop. The Home Office Citizenship Survey[6] was conducted for the first time in 2001 and repeated in 2003 and 2005. It examined social and civic participation in community life together with levels of formal and informal volunteering.

Civic participation, formal volunteering and informal volunteering *over the previous 12 months*

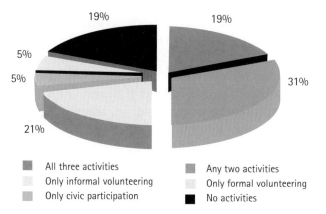

■ All three activities	■ Any two activities
Only informal volunteering	Only formal volunteering
■ Only civic participation	■ No activities

Source: 2005 Citizenship Survey, Department for Communities & Local Government

Schools today actively encourage volunteering, but the Institute for Voluntary Research discovered in 1997 that young adults were the least likely to volunteer. Whereas their involvement had declined since 1991, there has been a sharp rise in volunteering among those over 65.[7] This result agrees with the American evidence interpreted by Putnam. Many people are now beginning to value the personal benefits that come from volunteering, as Community Service Volunteers discovered in a survey of employees who do voluntary work organized through their workplace. They found that over half (53%) of these employees felt more productive, 18% felt healthier and had taken fewer days' sick leave, while 88% felt it had improved staff morale.[8] Volunteering in the workplace is a new concept to many employers, but on this evidence, one they should be taking seriously. It will be interesting to observe in the coming years how the phenomena of *Bowling Alone* in America translate into a British experience.

One additional aspect of the Home Office Citizenship Survey is its analysis involving social characteristics. Like Putnam, the survey found that education, socioeconomic grouping and favourable attitudes about their neighbourhood all predispose people towards volunteering. Also like Putnam, it found that both informal and formal volunteering were more likely to be undertaken by those who actively practised a religion. Charitable giving was more likely among people who actively practised a religion, and there was a strong positive association between giving money to charity and participation in voluntary activities. The Institute for Voluntary Research in a further report concluded that 'members of faith communities often grow up in a culture where it is the norm to 'help out'.[9] It acknowledged the large numbers of members who volunteer regularly and the wide range of voluntary activities that faith communities carry out, often with little external support. Figures from the Charity Commission reinforce these findings: 1 in 7 charities in England and Wales has a religious core and these 24,000 faith-based organizations have a combined income of £5.12 billion. 88% of faith-based organizations are Christian, and over the past 15 years the number of new Christian organizations have more than trebled so that they now make up a tenth of all new charities.

The contribution churchgoers make towards social capital and community life in Britain has only recently begun to be properly recognized. In 1999 Professor Robin Gill examined data from the British Household Panel Survey and concluded that members of religious groups were more than three times more likely to be involved in voluntary service than other people.[10] He conjectured that increasing secularity might fragment communities and reduce voluntary service associated with churchgoers, who are 'distinctive in their attitudes and behaviour'. The Bishop of Shrewsbury, Alan Smith, demonstrated this well in a piece of research among members of parochial church councils across rural Shropshire in 2002 and 2003. The results were compared with national findings from the British Social Attitudes Survey (2001).[11] In terms of membership of community organizations, membership of environmental organizations, social trust and neighbourliness, Shropshire PCC members consistently scored higher than the national average.

In 2001 the English Church Life Profile survey of churchgoers also found comparable results across Protestant churches. High levels of (inward-looking) *bonding* social capital were instanced by 58% of regular churchgoers having a role in the local church and nearly two-thirds belonging to small groups within the congregation.[12] High levels of (outward-looking) *bridging* social capital through community involvement beyond the church membership were evident:

> 21% are involved in social action through their congregation
>
> 24% are involved in service outside their congregation
>
> 22% have a position of responsibility in their community
>
> 61% donate to non-religious causes

Church attenders generate significant levels of *bonding* and *bridging* social capital. Dr Helen Cameron, in her analysis of these results, reports that church attenders who are engaged in social action are younger and less well educated than other community activists, they attend church more frequently, are more likely to donate to charity and are active in a range of church roles.[13] She concludes that the church evokes 'exceptional levels of activism from its members', making comparisons with two of the fastest growing membership organizations in the UK, namely the National Trust and the Royal Society for the Protection of Birds, that attract 1.5% and 8% respectively of their members into volunteering. The Church Life Profile estimated that 4 in 10 churchgoers undertake voluntary work each month outside their church, contributing 23.2 million hours a month of voluntary service, while a similar proportion undertake

voluntary work within their church, making a slightly smaller
contribution of 20.7 million hours a month to their churches.

More recently, two academic studies have focused in turn on rural
churches and on the Methodist Church. Faith in Rural Communities
Valuing Social Capital was a study led by Professor Richard Farnell of
Coventry University, supported by UK government department DEFRA
and the Arthur Rank Centre. One of its key findings is that people who
attend church regularly make a significant contribution to community
vibrancy, both through their engagement with church-based activity
and through their roles in village life more generally. They found
considerable evidence that people who are involved in church also
volunteer to lead or help organize a wide range of other activities in
village life such as the parish council, the Women's Institute and the
village hall. They also contribute informally through giving time to care
for others and help them enjoy a better quality of life. One interviewee
commented that people involved in the church 'are the ones with the
motivation to do things in the village . . . They are the ones who push
and drive and build the community. Without it the village would be
dead really.'[14] The study found others in rural communities who make
vital contributions but who do not share the faith of churchgoers, and
it commented too that contributions were most often made by older
people, which reflected the age structure of many rural communities.

Similarly, the Social Research Centre at Roehampton University
conducted a survey of Methodist churches across Britain in 2005
to examine how their congregations were involved in their
communities.[15] They found high stocks of social capital among
Methodist congregations, particularly in terms of civil participation
and volunteering. 93% of Methodists gave unpaid formal help over
the previous twelve months, compared with 44% from the 2005
Citizenship Survey. Methodists emerged as more engaged in the
community than the population at large. Furthermore, the results of
this research tend to suggest a breakdown of the distinction between
bridging and *bonding* social capital in that Methodists are equally
concerned with both.

So then, Christian churches, for their part, still see their local neighbourhood and their involvement in it as integral to their existence. They can often bring a younger vibrancy to comm-unity life. Ann Morisy, when Community Ministry Adviser for the Diocese of London, observed that 'the development of community ministry is an important contribution to becoming an authentic Church and authentic Christians'.[16] People of faith have the motivation to participate in the communal life of their neighbourhoods, and research shows that they make a difference for the good. Morisy cautions churches to ensure that their own aims in getting involved in community ministry are not taken over by the aims of those outside, but challenges churches to continue to see community ministry projects as a stepping stone between church and people, a means by which to bridge the gap.

Sacred presence

Churches and their buildings contribute to their local communities by their very presence. They speak, whether the message is of vibrant life, accessibility, struggling existence or former glories. Canon Professor Grace Davie acknowledges the 'symbolic importance of the church building both for the community of which it is part and, in many cases, for the wider public'.[17] Although most people in Britain do not attend their local churches with any regularity, they feel strongly about the church buildings present in their locality and frequently protest when a building is threatened with closure.

How the public relate to their church buildings is an interesting phenomenon. Professor William Storrar describes the restoration of one particular church back into a sacred space for the local community.[18] By the late 1990s the dwindling number of ageing church members were struggling to survive when a new minister redeveloped the dilapidated church building and halls into new forms of ministry.

MORISY CAUTIONS CHURCHES TO ENSURE THAT THEIR OWN AIMS IN GETTING INVOLVED IN COMMUNITY MINISTRY ARE NOT TAKEN OVER BY THE AIMS OF THOSE OUTSIDE, BUT CHALLENGES CHURCHES TO CONTINUE TO SEE COMMUNITY MINISTRY PROJECTS AS A STEPPING STONE BETWEEN CHURCH AND PEOPLE, A MEANS BY WHICH TO BRIDGE THE GAP.

A community café and a professional counselling centre were established alongside a chapel of remembrance, a food co-operative and a second-hand goods store. So the church building was transformed into 'an open, welcoming place where local people belong and find hope for their lives and communities', and thus memories and associations once more became attached to the church building. It redeveloped its role as a sacred presence in the neighbourhood.

Corporate memories are frequently preserved in our local churches and cathedrals. As a nation Britain is once more coming to value its heritage, a considerable amount of which is tied up in church buildings, for approaching half (45%) of all grade 1 listed buildings are Church of England churches. In November 2005 English Heritage discovered that over two-thirds (68%) of adults in Britain feel that 'places of worship reflect our historic legacy'. Churches are not today the way of life they once were, but they make vital contributions to social connectedness and they frequently reflect the historic memory of their local community. The challenge for local churches and cathedrals is how to make this inherited role relevant to their modern-day neighbourhood, so that the sacred presence they bring comes to fuller life once more.

St James the Less, London

4

Surprising signs of the times

Amid the challenge of community life that is gradually becoming disconnected and fragmented, Professor Robert Putnam and others are uncovering hopeful signs of community renewal.[1] Churches are frequently involved in some way in such stories. Visiting local homes, distributing church magazines, organizing open-air services, holiday clubs, young people's football teams – these and much more are all regular features in the life of many churches. The Revd Dr Alison Morgan of ReSource Ministries writes about the ways in which the gospel engages with contemporary life. She encourages churches to recover a deeper social faith through praying for their communities:

> So it is open to us to be part of the life-changing purposes of God. We will never fully experience the reality of his kingdom on this earth, for all these things are meant to be to us as signs . . . every transformed community remains subject to the forces which seek to destroy it.[2]

Churches that have taken this challenge seriously have found new life where before prospects were bleak. 'Listening to the nation' and 'Listening to the local' have shown us the need in the lives of our neighbours for things churches can offer. They have also shown us that our churches continue to be valued as part of everyday individual and community life. We now turn to some 'Surprising signs of the times' that churches have uncovered when they have taken their life within society seriously.

Open all hours

By 'Listening to the local' we have discovered the key role that open churches can have in the lives of local residents and visitors. The impact of a church on its surrounding neighbours is seriously eroded when its doors are shut, even if the key is available nearby. It takes considerable motivation to find a way into a church or any other building if the times of opening are spasmodic or the address given for the key holder remains a mystery. What greets the visitor is a serious deterrent.

I<small>T TAKES</small>
C<small>ONSIDERABLE</small>
M<small>OTIVATION</small>
T<small>O FIND A</small>
W<small>AY INTO</small>
A <small>CHURCH</small>
O<small>R ANY OTHER</small>
B<small>UILDING IF</small>
T<small>HE TIMES OF</small>
O<small>PENING ARE</small>
S<small>PASMODIC OR</small>
T<small>HE ADDRESS</small>
G<small>IVEN FOR THE</small>
K<small>EY HOLDER</small>
R<small>EMAINS A</small>
M<small>YSTERY.</small>

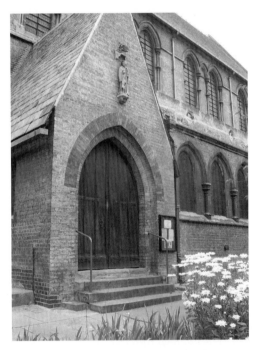

Daytime closure in a busy town

A couple enquiring about a church wedding visited their local church on five occasions to talk with someone but on each occasion found the doors shut and no means to make contact.

Not surprisingly, they decided it would be easier to have their wedding elsewhere and the church lost an opportunity to make contact with a local couple! Many churches have problems finding people willing to ensure a welcoming and safe presence during opening hours, but even that has been said by insurance companies not to be an insurmountable problem. Case histories indicate that buildings that are open to their communities, in regular use and loved by them are less likely to be burgled and vandalized. Of course, there are times when churches do have to close their doors, but even then there are ways of creating the impression of an open and hospitable church.

St Saviour's Church, London

Sadly, our churches have lost their reputation for hospitality. Consider the following comments made in a newspaper article focusing on the changing roles of pubs and churches:

> Nowadays, the church is open one Sunday in four . . . Indeed, pubs and churches have swapped roles . . . One survey . . . found that almost two thirds of Britons believe a hostelry has more to offer them than a house of God . . . if it is communion you want, the confidences at the bar flow more freely than at the altar rail.[3]

IF WE ARE TO ATTRACT A WIDER CLIENTELE TO OUR CHURCHES WE MUST 'MAKE CASUAL CUSTOMERS (EVEN ONES WITHOUT A CLUBCARD) FEEL THAT IT IS THEIR SORT OF PLACE'.

The journalist David Self found himself visiting a number of churches across the summer of 2006 and wrote of his experience under the title 'Church mislays its welcome mat'.[4] He found notices of services on the church gate a mystery (8 a.m. HC BCP; 10.30 SE CW Order One) and the notices shared during the service to be a 'members only' zone for a private club rather than a branch of a worldwide Church. At one church he was told that coffee after the service was only for regulars! He not only lamented the lost 'art of window-dressing' but sounded a warning that if we are to attract a wider clientele to our churches, we must 'make casual customers (even ones without a Clubcard) feel that it is their sort of place'.

The church of Caister St Edmund near Norwich took this seriously, and on Sunday afternoons during the summer of 2006 opened its doors. Visitors were welcomed by a member of the congregation and light refreshments were available. The success of this led to the church's being open throughout Open Churches Week in August. Four hundred people visited the church, many for the first time. Some took time to sit and be quiet, others were interested in the history of the building, while young visitors enjoyed filling in worksheets.

Open churches can also be a means by which churches tackle the problem of funding their buildings. English Heritage has commented on the growing number of buildings that are falling out of use because of changes needed for modern facilities. Churches are not alone in wrestling with this problem, but closing down is not the solution. St Leonard's Church, Bilston, a town centre church in an urban priority area of the West Midlands, opened its doors and found that it wiped out their financial deficit and increased and extended the congregation in the process. The rector, the Revd Chris Thorpe, reflected:

> A lot of it was unexpected. We didn't plan the café – it just happened. We opened up the church, and two hundred people a week just come in and pray. You can plan missions, and how to get in touch with people, but sometimes I think we just need to open our doors and wait and see who comes, and what God does with them.[5]

This church set itself the target of opening the buildings for 60 hours a week, instead of six, by developing a series of church-run projects that could earn enough rental income to pay off its debts. It didn't want to become a community centre but to preserve its worship centre and be in the centre of the community. 'There is now not an inch of space', says Chris Thorpe, 'the church has become the focus for a lot of community meetings; so the regeneration of Bilston actually gets planned in St Leonard's . . . We haven't done a huge amount of alteration; they're just all over the church, which is wonderful'.

'Listening to the past ' has reminded us that cathedrals are frequently places where visitors explore their need for personal quiet and reflection, connecting with their own spirituality. Truro Cathedral controversially opened its Sunday evening worship to incorporate country and western music, jazz and poetry and even an Elvis Presley evening. Wakefield Cathedral designed its own spiritual journey commentary on a CD presentation to accompany

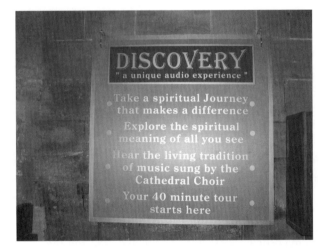

Wakefield Discovery Plaque

visitors around the cathedral. The Discovery tour helps people to appreciate the spiritual significance of different parts of the cathedral and at each stage they are invited to stop and reflect personally. At the rood screen, for example, a biblical passage is used; at the candle tree they are encouraged to offer prayers and at the choir to reflect on worship (to the music of the choir). The success of this CD has generated a take-home version and a children's version for school groups.

There are other ways of opening church doors into the community. In the companion booklet *Christian roots, contemporary spirituality* we became aware of the importance of prayer and spirituality in the lives of modern-day Britons. When churches open their doors, their particular situation may make them better placed to offer their own ways of encouraging visitors to pray and explore their own spirituality. As we saw in this companion booklet, prayer stations, prayer labyrinths, prayer boards and candles are each effective ways of providing such opportunities. Some churches have taken the idea of Christmas tree festivals (and, of course, flower festivals) mentioned there one stage further, for example, to create a Scarecrow festival around the time of

Prayer station at Wakefield Cathedral

harvest celebrations. Scarecrows are decorated and sponsored in aid of charity, new faces come into church and opportunities are offered for friendship and reflection. Churches that open their doors will find new life and creative thinking, but it will not be successful without careful planning and prayer. Stories of what God has done when churches open their doors have prompted the Bishop of London, Richard Chartres, to comment:

> The truth is that the Church is being re-imagined and recalled to its primary task – which is being with the people of England for the sake of God and with God for the sake of the people of England.[6]

CHURCHES THAT OPEN THEIR DOORS WILL FIND NEW LIFE AND CREATIVE THINKING, BUT THEY WILL NOT BE SUCCESSFUL WITHOUT CAREFUL PLANNING AND PRAYER.

Community churches

'Listening to the nation' and 'Listening to the local' have shown us how churches are valued by modern-day society as important parts of the local community. We saw how people want their churches to be more actively involved in their local community and to be more accessible. 'Listening to the past' has reminded us that although the role of the Church in society has changed in recent years, it still has a unique role to play. *Country Life* magazine sought to recognize the often unsung role of the priest in rural communities. Their competition resulted in some well-known finalists and some not so well-known, including the Revd Christine Musser, whose church played an important part in the aftermath of flash floods in Boscastle, and the Revd Timothy Jones, who gave spiritual leadership to the people of Soham following the murders of Holly Wells and Jessica Chapman.[7] Each was recognized for the unique contribution he or she (and their local congregations) had made to local community life. For the Church's part, if it is to make people feel more comfortable when they come to church services it must build bridges into the lives of its neighbours and encourage people to use churches at other times. Bringing together these needs of both church and community is encouraging more and more churches to consider how they can get more involved in their neighbourhoods and how their church buildings can be used for the benefit of both church and community.

St Barnabas' Church, Adeyfield, Hemel Hempstead, for example, opens its church buildings for nine different children's and youth groups, including uniformed organizations. It hosts Bingo and befriending for the elderly, Druglink (a drug rehabilitation group) and Platoon (a special needs group). It has formed partnerships with various local agencies, schools and a nearby residential home. The Bromley-by-Bow United Reformed Church in Tower Hamlets, London was in contrast a church struggling

Country Life MAGAZINE SOUGHT TO RECOGNIZE THE OFTEN UNSUNG ROLE OF THE PRIEST IN RURAL COMMUNITIES.

with an underused building. Then in the 1980s it opened its doors to some artists to use the space as their studio. Instead of rent they agreed to run classes for local people. There is now a café, nursery, dance school and a range of adult education activities alongside a worship area.[8]

In rural areas, churches, pubs, post offices and village shops are growing together to form 'community hubs'. Churches meeting in pubs may not be new, but All Saints, Sheepy Magna, Leicestershire hosts the post office and small shop, while the Vicar of St James' Church, Hemingford Grey, Cambridgeshire doubles as the village sub-postmaster. The Revd Peter Cunliffe has noticed several gains from this community-minded approach to church life:

> We took the post office over three years ago as a non-profit-making business . . . It has been an invaluable part of our church life, as people come into the hall to the post office, where we also have a church receptionist to welcome people.[9]

IN RURAL AREAS, CHURCHES, PUBS, POST OFFICES AND VILLAGE SHOPS ARE GROWING TOGETHER TO FORM 'COMMUNITY HUBS'.

Both ventures bring the churches into contact with many more people who, as one person commented, 'never darken the doors of a church'. The very rural church of St James, Welland was only open for an hour each week on Sundays when the parishioners in the area met to ask themselves where their churches were going and what the local needs were. They agreed that the greatest need was for their local teenagers, who had nowhere to go. So they applied to the Local Network Fund and received a grant to turn the neglected undercroft of St James' Church into a drop-in centre for young people. The young people helped with the decorating and devised their own rules of conduct to form a small clubroom they variously describe as 'cool' and 'wicked'.[10]

Since 1985 a strong thread of the work of Christchurch, Bridlington has been community programmes and developing a strong community base. This is a large church that supports an under-fives second-hand clothes, toys and equipment shop, a furniture store and a debt help centre. These ventures have led the church into a pre-school ministry and a ministry among the homeless. Seeking to reach other areas of the community, the church began The Bridge café in a converted derelict building. In time, guitar classes were being organized, a football team formed and from all this came the establishment of a church plant, Spotlight Church.[11] Of course, community involvement can also be effective with a lower-key approach, as some churches found when they started to provide informal morning 'tea and toast' sessions for people to call in at the start of the day.

St Peter's Church, Shipley wanted to plant a church in nearby Hirst Wood, but its vision was for a community church. Unit 8 community church on the industrial estate became the home to different youth clubs on Mondays, Tuesdays and Wednesdays, incorporating prayer and worship.[12] It grew an older people's club on Tuesday afternoons, a Guardian and Toddler group and a Thursday Homework club (in partnership with the Titus Salt Foundation Trust). Gradually, links have been formed to homes and families in an area of the parish where St Peter's had no presence. By building community, they hope not just to build a congregation but a church. A similar situation came about at Grange Park, Northamptonshire but with one major difference – there was no church building. So the church seeks to reach out into this new estate by meeting for worship in the local community centre and less formally in people's homes. A group for new mums and their babies and a monthly midweek group to tell Bible stories to pre-schoolers and their carers, for example, have led to an evening group for adult enquirers. The minister's wife explains:

COMMUNITY INVOLVEMENT CAN ALSO BE EFFECTIVE WITH A LOWER-KEY APPROACH, AS SOME CHURCHES FOUND WHEN THEY STARTED TO PROVIDE INFORMAL MORNING 'TEA AND TOAST' SESSIONS FOR PEOPLE TO CALL IN AT THE START OF THE DAY.

Unit 8 community church, Hirst Wood

Having or not having a church building is not an issue. The church is freed up in many ways and able to think creatively ... We focus on being part of the community of Grange Park; to go out to the people rather than imagine they might like to come to us. We contribute to anything good that goes on in the community, whether it is community fireworks or helping at the school fête, and see our input as blessing what Jesus is already doing in Grange Park.[13]

St Martin's in Byker, Newcastle is a new church recently opened in a deprived area of Newcastle. In the first two months after its opening it was visited by over a thousand people. A third of the building has been kept as a worship area but flexible spaces mean the church can be used for all kinds of different purposes. Accommodation is currently provided for a nursery and a community centre for up to twenty organizations, classes and training. The Revd John Sadler is

pleased that 'there is a great sense of ownership by the community', but he points out that the congregation 'are beginning to feel that the church is no longer theirs to do what they want with'.[14] Community involvement frequently comes at a cost!

CHRISTIANS GO OUT ON TO THE STREETS AT NIGHT TO OFFER HELP AND ADVICE TO PEOPLE LEAVING PUBS AND CLUBS IN THE TOWN.

Of course, community-minded churches do not always have to offer their buildings for use by their neighbours. Bridport Church in Dorset has organized a helpline for people who need to be put in touch with social services or Benefits Agency staff. The charity Parish Nursing Ministries UK was launched in September 2006 to provide support to a growing number of churches wishing to develop whole-person health-care ministry in their community. A few years ago an East London parish started offering its worship services in Portuguese to welcome migrants from Portuguese- and Spanish-speaking countries. In that time its congregations have grown from a few hundred to a thousand or more. Churches in Lincolnshire are working together with their local police to establish Prayer Watch initiatives. Prayer Watch works along the same principles as Neighbourhood Watch but it provides the added spiritual dimension of prayer for local issues and victims. It fosters close liaison between churches in a neighbourhood and the local police. The Bishop of Bath and Wells, Peter Price, recently launched a new Street Pastors scheme in Weston-super-Mare, Somerset. The interdenominational scheme is similar to schemes in several other UK cities and sees Christians go out on to the streets at night to offer help and advice to people leaving pubs and clubs in the town. They pray for the area, the pub and club staff, the police and the party-goers. The co-ordinator of the Kingston Street Pastors summed up their aims:

> To bring the love of God to those in need, to be
> a visible presence, not preaching, but loudly

proclaiming by our actions that the church is alive and
ready to serve the vulnerable.[15]

A commendable aim for any community-minded church!

Alternative communities

We live in a 24/7 society where people expect their amenities and local
services to be open all hours for their convenience. 'Listening to the
past' has reminded us that our churches are viewed as 'public spaces',
but it isn't always easy (or even desirable) to open our church buildings
on every occasion. The worldwide electronic revolution has changed
our shopping habits, our information habits, our leisure and education
habits, our communication habits and a whole lot more. Churches are
discovering that they can use these tools to change people's views on
church and for their church to be available out of hours. With creative
thought, there are endless opportunities for churches to communicate
through this means with their neighbourhoods and beyond.

St Margaret's Church, Streatley and St Mary's Church, Arnold
have both developed their own web sites to reflect the range of
activities hosted by their churches month by month.[16] St Mary's web
site, for example, currently 'advertises' an open church prayer day, a
firework party, a wine and wisdom evening, a coffee morning, a
Remembrance service and the turning on of the Christmas lights! It
provides links to separate information on children's activities, youth
work, adult groups, the church diary and church contacts. Baptism and
wedding enquirers can find answers to their initial questions, while
people wanting to 'post a prayer', find prayer guidance or a daily Bible
verse can find help. The journalist Chris Rees, writing in the *Church
Times*, recommends this approach to churches and would take it further.

> We should work towards every parish having its
> own web site. Our ministers should be equipped
> with the skill and means to create an electronic equivalent
> of the monthly Letter from the Vicarage: the Vicar's Blog.[17]

Vicars who have seen this potential means of reaching people
who are unable to attend church have found their reflections
being appreciated far beyond their parish boundaries – even
on an international scale!

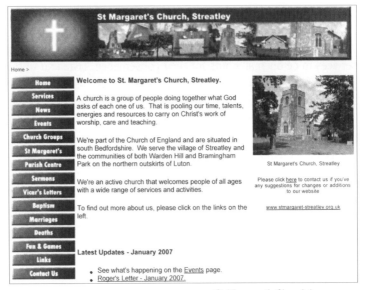

St Margaret's Church home page

The electronic boom also provides churches and other
organizations with the opportunity to reach people who are
disconnected from local churches not just by distance but by
intention. The Newcastle Methodist District and the ReJesus web
site are among those who have created an online labyrinth that
invites visitors on a spiritual journey of encounter and challenge.[18]
St Mary's Church, Ealing uses a specific web site to invite spiritual
searchers to their monthly Grace meetings on Saturday and
Sunday evenings at 8 p.m. The Ship of Fools 'magazine of
Christian unrest' is well known, but the Methodist Church has
sponsored an online church offering reflections, jokes and
discussion.[19] St Pixel's, as it is called, is an experiment in online

Lost in wonder online labyrinth

Christian community. Aligned to the modern monastic movement, the Pilgrim Community of Bangor Monochorum, an ecumenical internet community, had its first cyberspace day-retreat.[20] Members live all round the world, they live by a simple rule and a form of daily prayer while going about their daily life. They are a virtual community.

Dr Pete Ward of King's College, London, looks to a future world where community will be 'based on communication rather than gathering', where people will know each other but communicate electronically through mobile phones and other technology.

> Community would evolve around what people find interesting, attractive or compelling. A good example would be a spirituality based on the environment.[21]

The danger here, as Ward points out, is that the connections in such a community are 'based on a natural affiliation rather than on a sense of obligation or monolithic gathering', similar to that of a pressure group or particular activity. The Church cannot afford to restrict itself to any particular interest group, even though it should engage with technological advances. This salutary note was foreseen some years ago by the Tomorrow Project when it posed the question:

Greater affluence and better education is giving more choice over which communities to belong to. Fewer people are tied to the neighbourhoods where they were born. They have the freedom to move away, and to decide which clubs or groups to join. They link up with others on the basis of shared interest – and increasingly shared experiences. So are local communities giving way to communities of interest?[22]

Churches have frequently made connections with their local community through interest groups, but these interest groups present both opportunities and restrictions. Dr Norman Shiel, an Open University lecturer, studied the rise of football through the Victorian era and discovered that many football clubs were born out of church groups. Aston Villa, for example, started life as a group of Wesleyan churchgoers who took up football only to fill their time in the winter as they waited for the cricket season to begin. In many towns and villages of Britain today football is maintained by pub sides. 'Football is still the focus of a community, but that focus has moved away from the church, which in many ways is a shame.'[23] Professional football has outgrown its community roots but many clubs continue to value their chaplain or local minister.

Another example of alternative communities has always played a central role in community life. The links churches have with local schools are frequently taken for granted and deserve widespread celebration. Hereford Diocese conducted a survey of their parishes

Year 7 pupils exploring good and evil in the modern world

in 2005. They discovered that 42% of parishes had church representation on the board of school governors and that where the local church provides input into school assemblies, 61% do so on a weekly basis and 84% on a monthly basis or more frequently. Overall, church links with their local schools are strong, with some clergy helping in after-school clubs and other activities. And these opportunities are not just restricted to primary schools. Religious Studies lessons at The Grove School, New Balderton, Newark have benefited from help with explorations into spiritual and moral issues.

Schools are frequently open to involvement with their local churches. Two church members in rural Devon approached four local schools, two of which were church schools, to invite them to join in a big harvest celebration that would include a focus on the needs of children who live in areas of famine. Three of the schools joined in with enthusiasm. They each contributed a 20-minute musical or dramatic presentation and included prayers that the children had written. The celebration met many of the requirements of the National Curriculum, as well as being an act of worship that drew the schools

Hopscotch marathon with Christ Church, Manchester

and churches together. There are now plans for a holiday club involving all the local schools and churches. Christ Church, Davyhulme (a suburb of Manchester) sought to develop relations with its local schools by offering the services of a team of Christian artists. One school responded warmly and also got involved in a sponsored hopscotch marathon organized by the church.[24]

Schools can be a tremendous vehicle for good in any community, and many schools appreciate the support of their local church. One church school that took this very seriously was Southdale Church of England Primary, in Ossett, near Wakefield, where pupils are nearly all white. The teachers devised a 'class swap' with Warwick Road Primary, a nearby school where nearly all the pupils are Asian and 100% are Muslim. During the scheme 8- and 9-year-old pupils spent a day a week at each other's schools, learning about religious and cultural festivals. At the end of the scheme, the two schools held a celebratory festival for parents and pupils at a local Muslim centre. The schools admit that this programme has helped both to widen the pupils' horizons and to tackle the problems of segregated communities.[25]

Churches can reach different parts of their local communities through their local schools. The church at Sutton-at-Hone and Horton-Kirby, near Dartford, found that its family services on Sundays and during the week were not particularly successful, so the vicar decided to move into the local school and started an after-school service there. Although the church and school were in the same road, he discovered a world of difference. People volunteered to help, and after six months there was a regular congregation of 55. With the retirement of the vicar, things waned, but the new vicar was keen to re-establish the venture and has also developed termly services held in church. The involvement of the children and their parents in church life has developed into children's groups that meet in the school on Sundays and come into church towards the end of the services.[26]

When schools and churches work together to build local communities, the result can be very helpful to both. If your local school uses your church building for worship or lessons, you already have a relationship that can be built on. Congregation members could be there to welcome; links could be made for Education Sunday and invitations to carol services, an Easter service or leavers' service offered.

Christ Church Primary at St Leonard's-on-Sea is unusual in that it seeks to be church at school, an alternative community church. The school is located at the centre of an urban priority area and organizes a communion service twice a term. What marks this school out is that these services are run by the children alongside their regular school collective and weekly class worship. They write the prayers, plan drama and readings, lead and sometimes compose the music. Older children wishing to receive communion are prepared by the local clergy, with a member of staff being a sponsor and prayer partner. The school's intake is multi-ethnic; 28 languages are spoken. Many youngsters come from deprived homes, are fostered or in care. There is very little bullying and suspensions are rare. The ethos is to be Christ to one another. The children recognize the school as a safe place where each person is valued. Past pupils and parents turn to staff and clergy at times of need and large numbers attend the end of year Eucharist. The school and church partnership has created a new church community.[27]

NOT ONLY IS MODERN-DAY BRITAIN BEGINNING TO VALUE ITS CHRISTIAN ROOTS ONCE AGAIN, BUT IT VALUES ITS LOCAL CHURCHES.

Towards a future

I hope that these 'Surprising signs of the times' have encouraged you to consider the *community value* of your church in a new light. As society changes at an ever-faster pace, so the nature of living, and living in community, is changing. Churches that take 'Time to listen' to the changes in their neighbourhoods and respond positively to them will find their own mission enhanced. Churches live in community with their neighbours, and the heartening news is that their presence is welcomed there. They have a unique role at the heart of local neighbourhoods. Not only is modern-day Britain beginning to value its Christian roots once again,[28] but it values its local churches. Churches in turn play a vital part in local neighbourhoods, attracting all sorts of people on all sorts of occasions. They are altogether places created by the people for the people. They can bring added value to their communities with signs of community life that may be counter-cultural.

Send us out in the power of your Spirit
to live and work to your praise and glory. Amen.[29]

Notes

Series introduction

1. *Evangelism in a Spiritual Age*, Church House Publishing, 2005.
2. Vincent Donovan, *Christianity Rediscovered*, Orbis, 1978, 2003.
3. John Paul II, 'Discourse to the Plenary Assembly of the Pontifical Council for Culture', 18 March 2004, quoted by Trystan Owain Hughes, *Anvil* 22(1), 2005.
4. J. V. Taylor, *The Go-Between God*, SCM Press, 1973.
5. David Ison (ed.), *The Vicar's Guide*, Church House Publishing, 2005.
6. Clive Marsh, *Christianity in a Post-Atheist Age*, SCM Press, 2002.
7. *Mission-shaped Church*, Church House Publishing, 2005.

Chapter 1 Listening to the nation

1. Office for National Statistics, 2005.
2. Defra, UK; Rural Affairs – Rural Strategy 2004/5.
3. *Focus on Older People*, Information Bulletin 14, Church Army, July 2006.
4. Commission on Urban Life and Faith, *Faithful Cities*, Church House Publishing and Methodist Publishing House, 2006.
5. *Wealth of the Nation 2006*, Information CACI Solutions; www.caci.co.uk
6. Gallup Polls UK for the European Values Study, 1990.
7. 'A Life of Leisure and Personal Aspiration in Europe', in *Vision for the Future Foundation*, January 2006.
8. Populas national survey for the *Times* newspaper, November 2004.
9. Office for National Statistics, 2006.
10. The Future Foundation 2005, www.future.foundation.net
11. Office of the Deputy Prime Minister, March 2006.
12. Social Trends 36, Office for National Statistics, 2006.
13. National poll by TNS for Google, March 2006.
14. YouGov poll, August 2006,
15. Social Trends 35 and 36, Office for National Statistics, 2005 and 2006.
16. National Statistics, May 2005.
17. *Faithful Cities*, Report from the Commission on Urban Life and Faith.
18. Keith Ward, *Faith in a Post-Modern World*, Gresham College lecture, April 2006.
19. Chris Baker and Hannah Skinner, *Faith in Action*, William Temple Foundation, 2006.

20. Discussed further in Lynda Barley, *Christian Roots, Contemporary Spirituality*, Church House Publishing, 2006

21. David Ison (ed.), *The Vicar's Guide*, Church House Publishing, 2005.

22. ICONS – A Portrait of England – www.ICONS.org.uk

23. Opinion Research Business, November 2005 for English Heritage and the Archbishops' Council, Church of England.

24. Opinion Research Business, October 2003 for Archbishops' Council, Church of England.

Chapter 2 Listening to the local

1. CommunicateResearch for Evangelical Alliance and Premier Radio, *What's God doing?* National online poll of 2,000 adults in Britain, January 2006.

2. *The Power and Potential of Well-being Indicators*, New Economics Foundation, 2004.

3. Gwyther Rees, Leslie J. Francis and Mandy Robbins, *Spiritual Health and the Well-Being of Urban Young People*, The Commission for Urban Life and Faith, The University of Wales, Bangor and The Children's Society, 2006.

4. Office for National Statistics, 2003.

5. *Out of Time*, TUC Annual Report 2006.

6. *Growing Older: Quality of Life in Old Age*, Open University Press, 2004.

7. Office for National Statistics, 1 September 2006.

8. National poll by Opinion Research Business for BBC Soul of Britain, 2000.

9. Time to Listen research, Timebank 2005.

10. *Trends in Geographical Mobility in Britain*, Tony Champion for PIU Strategic Thinkers Seminar, June 2002.

11. 'We didn't look fools after all', Bryony Gordon in the *Daily Telegraph*, 11 August 2005.

12. *British Social Attitudes, The 19th Report*, The National Centre for Social Research, Sage Publications, 2002.

13. Church Life Profile 2001, Churches Information for Mission.

14. Philip J. Richter and Leslie J. Francis, *Gone But Not Forgotten*, Darton, Longman & Todd, 1998.

15. Discussed further in Lynda Barley, 'Listening to the local', *Churchgoing Today*, Church House Publishing, 2006.

16. Survey of 500 regular churchgoers by Spring Harvest and Care for the Families, August 2005.

17. Church Life Profile, 2001, Churches Information for Mission.

18. Alan Gilchrist, *Culture of Welcome in the Local Church*, Grove Books, 2004.

19. Opinion Research Business, national poll for Archbishops' Council, Church of England, November 2005.

20. *Hello* magazine, July 2005.

21. Discussed in 'Listening to the nation', Lynda Barley, *Churchgoing Today*, Church House Publishing, 2006.

22. Opinion Research Business national opinion poll for Archbishops' Council, Church of England, November 2005.

23. Church Tourism Evaluation – Yorkshire Tourist Board, March 2005.

24. Further examination of church tourism is given by Trevor Cooper in *How do we Keep our Parish Churches?* Ecclesiological Society, 2004.

25. Derby Diocesan Council for Social Responsibility, *Faith in Derbyshire*, April 2006.

26. *Being Here: How the Church is Engaging with the Communities of Brighton and Hove*, Engage, The Brighton and Hove Churches Community Development Association, 2004.

27. *Organized Religion in East London*; www.astoncharities.org.uk/research/religion

28. *Your Cathedral: A Mission Audit Report for Wakefield Cathedral*, 2001.

29. *Listening for Mission: Mission Audit for Fresh Expressions*, Church House Publishing, 2006.

30. The Barking Road Community Audit, Aston-Mansfield Communities Involvement Unit 2001.

31. www.cuf.org.uk/resources

Chapter 3 Listening to the past

1. Timothy Jenkins, *Religion in English Everyday Life*, Berghahn Books, New York, 1999.

2. See, for example, *Christianity and Social Service in Modern Britain*, Frank Prochaska, 2006.

3. For example, Douglas Davies, Charles Watkins and Michael Winter, *Church and Religion in Rural England*, T&T Clark, 1991; Leslie J. Francis, *Rural Anglicanism*, Collins 1985; Douglas Davies, 'Priests, Parish and People: Reconceiving a Relationship' in Martin Guest, Karin Tusting and Linda Woodhead (eds), *Congregational Studies in the UK*, Ashgate, 2004.

4. Figures collated in Robin Gill, *The Empty Church Revisited*, Ashgate, 2003.

5. Robert D. Putnam, *Bowling Alone: The Collapse and Revival of American Community*, Simon & Schuster, New York, 2000.

6. 2001, 2003, 2005 Citizenship Surveys, The Home Office and Office of the Deputy Prime Minister. Representative split samples of 14,000 adults aged 16 and over in England and Wales.

7. Institute for Voluntary Research national survey, 1997.

8. Community Service Volunteers survey of 200,000 staff in 11 organizations, 2005, www.csv.org.uk

9. *Faith and Community Action: community, values and resources*, Institute for Volunteering Research, 2003.

10. Robin Gill, *Churchgoing and Christian Ethics*, Cambridge University Press, 1999

11. Alan Smith writing in Martineau et al. (eds), *Changing Rural Life*, Canterbury Press, 2004.

12. Church Life Profile, Churches Information for Mission 2001.

13. Dr Helen Cameron, *The Community Involvement of Church Attenders: Findings from the English 2001 Church Life Profile*, 2002.

14. Richard Farnell et al., *Faith in Rural Communities: Contributions of social capital to community vibrancy*, Applied Research Centre for Sustainable Regeneration, Coventry University and Arthur Rank Centre, October 2006.

15. *Making a difference? Social capital and the Methodist Church*, Social Research Centre, University of Roehampton, September 2006.

16. Ann Morisy, *Beyond the Good Samaritan*, Community Ministry and Mission, Continuum, 1997.

17. Grace Davie, From *Obligation to Consumption: Patterns of religion in northern Europe at the start of the twenty first century*, University of Exeter, September 2004.

18. William Storrar, 'The Resources and People of the Local Church – Theological Strand' in Helen Cameron, Philip Richter, Douglas Davies and Frances Ward (eds), *Studying Local Churches*, SCM Press, 2005.

Chapter 4 Surprising signs of the times

1. See, for example, Robert Putnam and Lewis Feldstein, *Better Together*, Simon & Schuster Paperbacks, 2003.

2. Alison Morgan, *The Wild Gospel,* Monarch Books, 2004.

3. 'Inn fashion', Leading articles, the *Times,* 10 November 2004.

4. David Self, 'Church mislays its welcome mat', in *Church Times,* 25 August 2006.

5. Pat Ashworth, 'Open the door and they will enter, says St Leonard's' in *Church Times,* 27 May 2006.

6. Richard Chartres, 'Church coffers are half full, not half empty' in the *Times,* 18 June 2005.

7. Jonathan Petre and Jonathan Wynne-Jones, 'Country folk honour the good shepherds', in the *Daily Telegraph,* 19 October 2005.

8. Reported in the Ann Morisy, *Beyond the Good Samaritan,* Continuum, 1997.

9. Reported in the *Church Times*, 22 December 2006.

10. Reported in Margaret Duggan, 'Real Life' in the *Church Times*, 17 February 2006.

11. Information from research by The Sheffield Centre, Church Army.

12. *Unit 8: Out of sight, out of nothing – Encounters on the Edge*, The Sheffield Centre, Church Army.

13. 'Children at Grange Park Church', in Margaret Withers, *Mission-shaped Children*, Church House Publishing, 2006.

14. Reported in Margaret Duggan, 'Real Life', in the *Church Times*, 8 September 2006.

15. Reported in *The Bridge*, Southwark diocese newspaper, October 2006.

16. www.stmargaret-streatley.org.uk and www.stmaryarnold.org.uk

17. Chris Rees, 'Is this another innovation that the Church will miss?' the *Church Times*, 29 September 2006.

18. www.lostinwonder.org.uk and www.rejesus.co.uk

19. www.ship-of-fools.com and www.stpixels.com

20. Eva McIntyre, 'World's first web retreat?' the *Church Times*, 17 March 2006.

21. Pete Ward, *Liquid Church*, Paternoster Press, 2002.

22. Michael Moynagh and Richard Worsley, *Tomorrow*, May 2000.

23. Peter Taylor-Whiffen, 'Church and pubs led to football clubs', *Open Eye Magazine*, Spring 2002.

24. Margaret Duggan, 'Hopping for the hospice' in 'Real Life', in the *Church Times*, October 2006.

25. Matthew Taylor, 'Why are you wearing that on your head?' the *Guardian*, 22 August 2006.

26. Reported in Project REACH, Archbishops' Council, Mission and Public Affairs Division.

27. Margaret Withers, *Mission-shaped Children*, Church House Publishing, 2006.

28. See Lynda Barley, *Christian Roots, Contemporary Spirituality*, Church House Publishing, 2006.

29. *Common Worship: Holy Communion Order One*, Church House Publishing, 2000.

Acknowledgements

We are grateful to the following for permission to reproduce images in this book:

The Church Army, Sheffield Centre for the image of Unit 8 from *Encounters on the Edge*, Number 2 (page 53).

The Grove School, New Balderton, Newark for permission to photograph pupils during lessons (page 59).

The Revd Bob Hill for the Hopscotch image (page 28), which originally appeared in the *Church Times*.

The Revd Canon John Holmes for permission to use photographs from Wakefield Cathedral (pages 48 and 49).

Andy Stonehouse for the image of gated housing, copyright © Andy Stonehouse, 2006 (page 3).